BIRMINGH

IN THE

SIXTIES

VOL 2

Alton & Jo Douglas

Pershore Road/Hazelwell Lane, Stirchley, 27th October 1969.

ISBN 1 85858 147 8
Published by Brewin Books Ltd., Doric House, 56 Alcester Road, Studley, Warwickshire B80 7LG
Printed by Warwick Printing Co. Ltd., Theatre Street, Warwick CV34 4DR
Layout by Alton and Jo Douglas

The Law Courts, Corporation Street, 27th January 1964.

Front Cover: Bull Ring, April 1960.

C o n t e n t s

BREWIN BOOKS LTD

Doric House, 56 Alcester Road,
Studley, Warwickshire B80 7LG

Tel: 01527 854228   Fax: 01527 852746

Vat Registration No. 705 0077 73

Dear Nostalgic,

It's amazing how well people respond to a challenge! After "Birmingham in the Fifties" and "Birmingham in the Sixties" came out, several people wrote to us to say how much they'd enjoyed the books but that they had even better material themselves. Bristling, with ill-placed indignation, yours truly retorted, "O.K. – prove it!".
In reply, dust clouds rose in attics as tea-chests were opened for the first time in "donkey's ears" (well, that's what I thought it was when I was little), relatives were pestered, photographs prised out of albums and so on as the whole enterprise became a quest for that elusive better picture/leaflet/cutting – whatever. In parallel, with all that work, Jo and I set out on our personal excavations.

This book, along with "Birmingham in the Fifties Vol. 2", is the result of that partnership between you and us. I hope you think it was worthwhile – we do!

Yours, in friendship,

Alton

St Martin's Place, between Broad Street and Cambridge Street, 13th July 1961.

An accident with a crane means the traffic is diverted the wrong way down a one-way street, Albert Street, 19th January 1960.

SHOWBOAT

THE CAKE IN A CHOCOLATE SHELL BY

KUNZLE

everyone's fancy
for every occasion

John Bright Street, with Station Street in view,
10th February 1960.

Shirley Road, Acocks Green, February 1960.

Heathfield Service Station, Heathfield Road, Handsworth, 16th February 1960.

Coleshill Road, Ward End, 23rd February 1960.

Washwood Heath Road, March 1960.

Stratford Road, Sparkhill, 1960.

Transport Minister, Ernest Marples, M.P., chats to spectators at the opening of the first section of the
Inner Ring Road, 11th March 1960.

Woodbridge Road/Alcester Road, Moseley, 1960.

Station Road, with Lyndon Road on the right, Stechford, 31st March 1960.

Richmond Court, George Road, Edgbaston,
20th April 1960.

Green Lane/Redvers Road, Small Heath, 21st April 1960.

Cherrywood Road, Bordesley Green, 1960.

Monument Road/Ledsam Street, Ladywood, 21st April 1960.

Birmingham and other Midland police officers are to launch an intensive campaign designed to cut the number of cars stolen in their areas and the number of thefts from vehicles.

Plans were announced yesterday when a Birmingham police official said that altogether 16 forces would be taking part. In recent months incidents involving cars have amounted to one in every nine of the total number of crimes reported to the police.

New warning posters are to be displayed at garages, car parks, sports grounds and outside public houses. Police officers will also distribute leaflets advising motorists to lock their vehicles and not to leave windows open or valuable articles inside.

Witton Lodge Road, Perry Common, 4th May 1960.

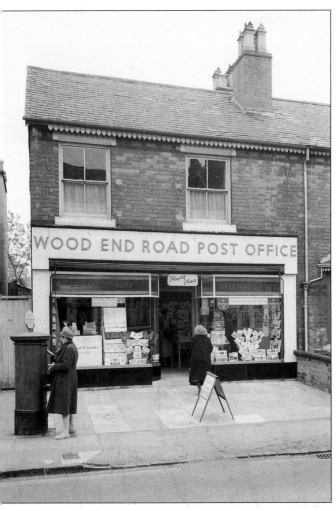

Wood End Road, Erdington, 20th May 1960.

Tommy Steele, the Rock-and-Roll singer who went on to become a world-class entertainer, takes part in a show biz football match, Perry Barr Stadium, 25th May 1960.

Chipperfield Road, Castle Bromwich, 25th May 1960.

Bridge Street West/Wheeler Street, Newtown, 30th May 1960.

Warwick Road/Reddings Lane, Tyseley, 31st May 1960.

Tyburn Road, Erdington, 30th June 1960.

Cadbury Bros. Ltd., Bournville Lane, c 1960.

The Bull Ring Market Hall, from Moor Street, July 1960.

Lea Hall Road, Yardley, 9th August 1960.

Rookery Road, Handsworth, 1960.

Hockley Hill, 16th August 1960.

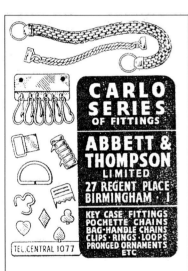

"Huckleberry Finn", Barford Road School, Rotton Park, c 1960.

The Lord Mayor and Lady Mayoress, Ald. and Mrs G.B. Boughton, take part in the annual civic inspection of the Wholesale Fruit and Vegetable Markets, 13th October 1960.

As a retirement celebration for City Treasurer, Mr J.P. Eames, a "This is your Life" presentation takes place, Council House, 22nd October 1960.

15

Highgate Street, 7th December 1960.

Lichfield Road, Aston, 1960.

1961

Kingstanding Road, January 1961.

Dudley Road, Winson Green, 5th January 1961.

Janet Barber (left) and Kath Jarvis at the rear of
Alice Owen's shop, Hick Street, Highgate, 1961.

Local M.P., Harold Gurden, begins a three day fact-finding
tour of the city's schools and meets boys from Selly Oak Boys'
School, Oak Tree Lane, 18th January 1961.

Lea Village, Kitts Green, 1961.

Birchfield Road, Newtown, 31st January 1961.

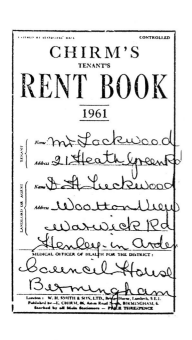

College Road, Kingstanding, 13th February 1961.

Calthorpe Road/St James' Road, Edgbaston, 17th March 1961.

The Lord Mayor, Ald. G.B. Boughton, receives the first licence to be
issued at the new Birmingham Taxation Offices, Oozells Street,
19th April 1961.

Court Road, from Edward Road, Balsall Heath, 29th May 1961.

Bordesley Green, 12th June 1961.

Manufactured by the Metropolitan-Cammel Carriage and Wagon Co. Ltd., the Blue Pullman arrives at Snow Hill Station, 1961.

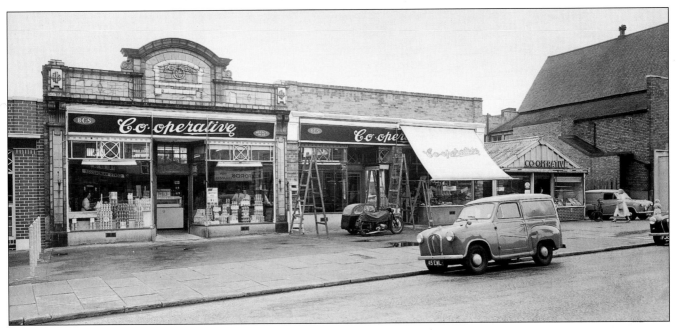

Station Road, Stechford, 12th July 1961.

Witton Road/Witton Lane, 25th July 1961.

Grant Street/Bell Barn Road, Edgbaston, 26th July 1961.

The Temperance Seven recording in the city, 15th July 1961. In April, of the same year, their record of "You're Driving Me Crazy" had been in the Top Ten. A decade later Alton appeared with the band in summer season, at the Pier Theatre, Shanklin, Isle of Wight.

THE BIRMINGHAM
REPERTORY THEATRE

In association with
THE ARTS COUNCIL OF GREAT BRITAIN

presents

on Tuesday, September 26th, 1961,
for four weeks

THE
CARETAKER

by

HAROLD PINTER

Characters in order of appearance:

MICK	DEREK JACOBI
ASTON	STEPHEN MACDONALD
DAVIES	ARTHUR PENTELOW

The Play directed by BERNARD HEPTON
Designed by DIANA DEWES

Betholom Row, between Bath Row and Islington Row, 30th August 1961.

Rear of 285 Coventry Road, Small Heath, 13th September 1961.

Walsall Road, Great Barr, 1961.

Suffolk Street/Station Street, 14th October 1961.

Dalton Street/James Watt Street, 14th October 1961.

The Camp Hill fly-over, in the rush hour, 17th October 1961.

Birchfield Road underpass scheme, 19th October 1961.

ON his way to work yesterday Alan Stearn called in to a betting shop and put a £2 accumulator on the favourites at Newbury.

On his way home he called in and collected his winnings —£1,289. For all his six selections won.

Mr. Stearn, 31 - year - old commercial artist of Leyhill Farm-road, Birmingham, has been "playing" the horses for about 10 years.

"All this week I'd been coming badly unstuck," he said last night. "Then today I decided to have a grand slam on the favourites. A two-quid accumulator—do or die."

Puffing at an outsize cigar he added: "I'm very glad I did."

Jimmy Powell and The Rockin' Berries, 19th October 1961.

Graham Street, Hockley, October 1961.

Yew Tree Lane/Church Road, South Yardley, 18th October 1961.

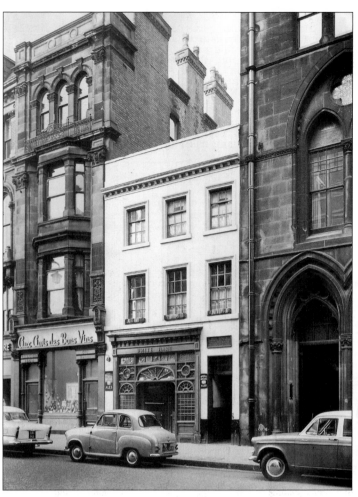

Two giants of the tenor sax – American, Zoot Sims (right) meets Tubby Hayes, Ronnie Scott Club (based at the Mermaid Hotel) Sparkhill, 20th November 1961.

Paradise Street, 21st November 1961.

Balsall Heath Road, with Longmore Street, on the left, 1961.

Bull Street, looking down from Corporation Street, 9th December 1961.

MAKE 1962 YOUR NEW FORD YEAR

Popular £517   Anglia £621   Classic £767   Consul £844   Zephyr £942   Zodiac £1,037

FORD POPULAR, 1957. Nice clean car. **£199**	FORD CONSUL, 1955. Extremely well kept. **£250**
FORD POPULAR, 1959. Spotless condition. **£250**	FORD CONSUL II, 1958. Magnificent con- dition **£465**
FORD POPULAR, 1959. Latest model. Fine value. **£369**	FORD CONSUL III, 1959. Low line. Special value! **£535**
FORD POPULAR D/L, 1959. Very smart car **£399**	FORD CONSUL III, 1960. Absolutely beautiful! **£595**
FORD ANGLIA, 1958. Blue, heater; 1 owner. **£335**	FORD CONSUL III, 1961. Disc brakes, radio, 10,000 miles. **£725**
FORD ANGLIA, 1961, New model. Choice of three. From— **£465**	FORD CONSUL II, 1960. 1 owner. Only 10,300 miles. **£645**
FORD ANGLIA D/L, 1958. Choice of four lovely cars. From— **£325**	FORD CONSUL D/L, 23,000 miles. Yellow/ black. **£555**
FORD ANGLIA D/L, 1959-61. Select from 12; all colours, with heaters. From— **£465**	FORD ZEPHYR III, 1959. Low mileage, exemplary condition. **£569**
FORD ANGLIA, 1958. Genuine 1-owner; 22,000 miles. **£345**	FORD ZEPHYR FARNHAM, 1958. Two-tone. Unmarked. **£599**
FORD ANGLIA D/L, 1956. Exceptional condition. **£285**	FORD ZODIAC, 1956-59 Choice of four nice cars. From— **£375**
FORD PREFECT D/L, 1959. Beautiful car; overdrive. **£399**	AUSTIN A35, 1957. Choice of three nice cars. From— **£285**
FORD PREFECT, 1959. Clean; low mileage. **£353**	AUSTIN A40, 1959. Genuine 18,000 miles. Red. **£460**
FORD PREFECT D/L, 1956. Fawn. Real beauty. **£295**	AUSTIN A55 D/L, 1959. Wonderful con- dition. **£495**
FORD PREFECT D/L, 1960, p.h.v. Yellow/ white. Almost new. **£485**	AUSTIN A55 D/L, 1960. Hide, heater, radio. 17,000 miles. **£650**
FORD SQUIRE ESTATE, 1958. Fawn, heater. Nice condition. **£325**	DAIMLER CONQUEST, 1953. Works engine, 5,000 miles. Outstanding condition. **£365**
FORD ESCORT ESTATE, 1960. One fastidious owner. **£399**	HILLMAN MINX D/L, 1959. Magnificent two-tone. **£525**

CAPRI £916

LET GO WITH THE NEW CAPRI —get the greater than ever thrill of FORD motoring—try it—buy it —at HANGERS

or choose a Better Used Car from our stock of over 250

Showrooms open until 7 p.m. weekdays, 6 p.m. Saturdays.

187, BROAD ST., B'HAM. 15. MID. 7131

214-5, BROAD ST., B'HAM. 15.

SIX WAYS, ERDINGTON, BIRMINGHAM, 23. ERD. 6206

FORD HANGERS DISTRIBUTOR

Depots Right Across Birmingham

Self-Financed Hire Purchase Terms available.

4-6, WOLVERHAMPTON ROAD, WARLEY. BEA. 4501

7, STEPHENSON ST., B'HAM. 2. MID. 3151

1161, CHESTER RD., CASTLE BROMWICH. ERD. 7401

Court Oak Road, Harborne, 2nd February 1962.

BOBBY VEE a popular young American singer now touring this country, lists cold weather as one of his chief dislikes.

When he arrived in Birmingham last night, a bitterly cold east wind swept around the Town Hall. But despite his views about the weather the one thing he will remember about the city is the tremendously warm reception he was given.

Mr. Vee has an extremely pleasant personality but unless you know his records, it was impossible to assess him as a singer at last night's shows.

Two pounding drum sets, three amplified guitars and two saxophones on stage, plus the hysterical screams, the hand-clapping and foot-stamping of the audience, completely drowned his voice.

The Pool, Meadow Hill Road, Kings Norton, 6th February 1962.

Public bowling green, Hazelwell Street, Stirchley, 1962.

Bell Lane, Tile Cross, March 1962.

Phil King and the Couriers load up the van after another successful gig, Gospel Oak, Gospel Lane, Acocks Green, 1962.

An
ORCHESTRAL CONCERT

by

The Birmingham Philharmonic Orchestra

GORDON RUSSELL *Baritone*
WENDY WILSON *Piano*

MICHAEL COLSTON *Associate Conductor*
KENNETH PAGE *Conductor*

*Presented by
Handsworth Round Table
at the Town Hall, Birmingham
Sunday, 4th March*

PROGRAMME : PRICE 6d.

Eight and a half hours of non-stop Rock 'n Twist, Town Hall, 30th March 1962.

BIRMINGHAM BACH SOCIETY

BACH
SAINT MATTHEW PASSION

SATURDAY
14th APRIL 1962

Part I 4.0 p.m.   Part II 7.0 p.m.

IN THE CATHEDRAL
by kind invitation of the Very Rev. the Provost

ADMISSION BY PROGRAMME 6/-
SCHOOLCHILDREN 3/-

Obtainable from : Choir Members,
Civic Radio Services Ltd.
or at the Door.

Rear of Wheeler Street, Newtown, April 1962.

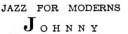

Scouts' Rally, Handsworth Park, c 1962.

Bunbury Road, at the traffic lights at The Bell Inn, Northfield (now the site of the
Grosvenor Shopping Centre), June 1962.

Turning right into Bristol Road South, after the previous photograph, we see
the well-known Hodgetts Pet Shop.

High Street, looking towards Dale End, c 1962.

Bull Ring, c 1962.

Bournville Village Green, Linden Road, 1962.

A specially designed van for H.P. Sauce Ltd., in the grounds of Aston Hall, 1962.

Moseley Secondary School of Art, 1962.

Geoffrey Lloyd, M.P. for Sutton Coldfield, about to embark on a tour of the Houses of Parliament, with pupils from Moor End School, Erdington, 10th July 1962.

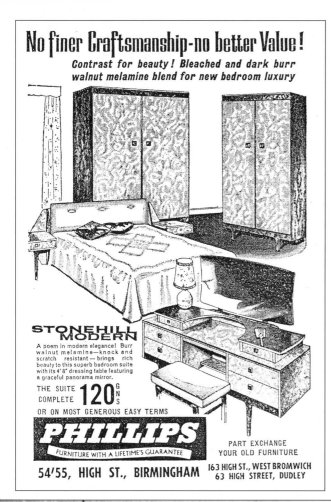

The front line of Dave Coles Jazz Band, 1962.

The staff of Stratford Road Primary School, Sparkbrook, 1962.

Fourth year juniors, Stratford Road Primary School, Sparkbrook, 1962.

Old Square, from Dale End, September 1962.

35

36

A break from "Robinson Crusoe" rehearsals for Norman Wisdom and five local dancers, Hippodrome, 11th December 1962.

The Johnny Everett Dixieland Band, Christmas 1962.

Colleen Avenue, Kings Norton, 1962.

Broadmeadow Infants' School, Kings Norton, 1962.

1963

Sir Edward Boyle, Minister of Education, talks to Raymond Pillinger in the Science Laboratory of the Harry Lucas Secondary School, Burbury Street, Lozells, 22nd January 1963.

Christmas party, Cromwell Hall, Evangelistic Mission Church, Heath Green Road, Winson Green, January 1963.

The building, that many Brummies hated, grows day by day, The Rotunda, January 1963. A quarter-of-a-century later there was a public outcry when it was suggested that it should be removed from Birmingham's skyline!

The Science Museum, Newhall Street, 1963.

Retirement party for John Renton (fourth from the left in the back row), Manager of the Yardley branch of Barclays Bank. The Barn, Hockley Heath, January 1963.

Court Oak Road/Wolverhampton Road South, Quinton, 25th February 1963.

St Paul's Square/Brook Street, Hockley, 25th February 1963.

Worcester Street, 5th March 1963.

CINEMATOGRAPH EXHIBITORS' ASSOCIATION
DON'T JUST GO OUT —
GO TO THE PICTURES !
Houses marked * denotes six-day programme.

ABC, Adelphi, Hay Mills.— Rory Calhoun, "Marco Polo" (U), 5.50, 9.5; "The Young and the Cool" (U). L.P. 7.20. Th.: 'Son of the Red Pirate' (U).

ALHAMBRA, Moseley Road.— Gregory Peck "The Bravados" (A) (Cont. 5.0 (Mon. 1.25). "The Enemy Below" (U) L.P. 6.50. Th.: "Blackboard Jungle" (x).

BEACON, Gt. Barr.— "Manchurian Candidate" (A), Frank Sinatra, Janet Leigh, 5.15, 8.10; Supporting programme: Thurs.: "My Bare Lady" (A).

BEAUFORT. — "Yesterday's Enemy" (A). 2.15, 5.29, 8.43 (Tues. 5.29); Supp. 3.50, 7.4 (Tu. 7.4). Ad. Th. 'Belles of St Trinians' U.

CAPITOL *—Judy Garland, Dirk Bogarde, "I COULD GO ON SINGING" (U); Sean Kelly, "GANG WAR" (A). Last performance 7.15.

CARLTON *, Taunton Road. Sparkbrook. Sou. 0861. Charlton Heston, Jack Hawkins, Stephen Boyd, 'Ben Hur' A. 6.55. once nightly. 5/-, 4/-, 3/-.

CLIFTON, Gt. Barr *— "Sodom and Gomorrah" (x) Stewart Granger, Pier Angeli, 4.40, 7.40 (Mon. 2.0). Full Support. L.P. 7.15. Adults.

CORONET.— " Camp On Blood Island " (x) 2.30, 5.45, 9.0; "Gunman's Walk" (A) 3.50, 7.5. Adults. Th.: The Warrior Empress' (U).

ABC, Edgbaston, Monument Road.—Don McGowan "Guns of the Black Witch" (A) 2.35, 5.50 9.0; "Phantom Planet" (U) L.P. 7.10. Th.: "Giant" (A).

EMPRESS, Sutton (A.B.C.).— A. Hepburn, H. Fonda "War and Peace" (U) 3.10, 7.10 (2 perf. only) L.P. 6.25. Th. "Man Who Knew Too Much" (A)

ESSOLDO, Longbridge. PRI. 2470.—"Vengeance of the Gladiators" (A) 2.14, 5.38, 9.7; Supp. L.P. 1.50 (Tue. 5.10). Th. "Blood of Vampire" (x)

ESSOLDO Cinema, Quinton * — "The Fast Lady" (A) 6.0, 9.0 (Mon. & Wed. 3.05); "Stranglehold" (A) 4.40, 7.35 (Mon. & Wed. 1.45).

GAIETY, Coleshill St. (ABC). "Iron Maiden" (U), 1.40, 5.15, 8.55; Supp. (U), 3.20, 7.0 (Mat. Mon only). Th. "Harold Lloyd's World of Comedy" (U)

GAUMONT * SME. 0950.— Dirk Bogarde, Judy Garlande "I Could Go On Singing" (U) 8.45 (Mat. M. & W. 2.25, 5.35); Supp. A. 7.15 (Mat. 4.10).

GROVE, Dudley Road *—Ian Hendry, June Ritchie, "Live Now, Pay Later" (x), 2.10, 5.20, 8.30; "Tell Tale Heart" (x) 3.55, 7.5. L.P. 7.5 Adults.

ABC, Handsworth. — Elvis Presley "WILD IN THE COUNTRY" (A), "The Street With No Name" (A). Comm. 2.35 L.P. 6.30. Th.: "Giant" (A).

IMPERIAL, Moseley Rd. (ABC). "Diary of a Nudist" (A), 5.50, 9.10; "Preludes to Ecstasy" (x), 5.10, 7.10. 7.10. Adults. Th.: "300 Spartans" (U).

KING'S NORTON. KIN. 1079. "The Premature Burial" (x), 5.45, 8.55 (Mon. 2.30); "Ordered to Love" (A) L.P. 7.10. Th.: "The Vikings" (A).

KINGSTON *—Judy Garland. "I COULD GO ON SINGING" (U) 2.43, 5.43, 8.43 "GANG WAR" (A) 4.27, 7.27.

KINGSWAY, King's Heath.— "I COULD GO ON SINGING" (U) Judy Garland, 2.20, 5.26, 8.37 "GANG WAR" (A) 4.0, 7.11. L.P. 7.11.

MAYFAIR, Perry Common * "BEN HUR" (A). D.O. 6.30. Screened at 6.45 (Mon. 2.0).

MOSELEY P.H. — Ben Gazzara, Stuart Whitman, "Reprieve" (A); Howard Keel, "Armoured Command" (A). Th.: "Prisoner of the Iron Mask" (U).

OAK, Selly Oak * (A.B.C)— Judy Garland, Dirk Bogarde, "I Could Go On Singing" (U), 2.05, 5.25, 8.45 "Gang War" (A) 3.50, 7.10, L.P.

ODEON, Perry Barr *—Judy Garland "I Could Go On Singing" (U), 2.25, 5.35, 8.45 (Cont. 2.0). "Gang War" (A). 4.5, 7.20. L.P. 7.20.

ODEON, Shirley * — Judy Garland, Dirk Bogarde, "I Could Go On Singing" (U), 2.15, 5.25, 8.40; "Gang War" (A). 4.0, 7.10

ODEON, Sutton *—"I Could Go On Singing" (U), 2.20, 5.35, 8.45; "Gang War" (A), 4.5, 7.18. L.P. 7.18.

OLTON *—" I Could Go On Singing " (U) Judy Garland, Dirk Bogarde; " Gang War " (A), Sean Kelly. L.P. 7.20.

ABC, Orient, Aston—Julie Martin "My Bare Lady" (A), 3.20, 6.20, 9.20; "Mam'selle Striptease" (A). 1.15, 4.15, 7.20. Th.: "Blackboard Jungle" (x)

PALACE, Erdington * (ABC). James Dean, Rock Hudson, Elizabeth Taylor. "GIANT" (A) 12.30, 3.55, 7.25. Th.: "FLAMING STAR" (A).

PALLADIUM, Hockley (ABC). —"Camp on Blood Island" (x), 5.40, 8.55; "Two Faces of Dr. Jekyll" (x), 4.0, 7.10. Ads. Th.: "Some Like it Nude" (A)

ABC, Pavilion, Stirchley.—Lex Barker, "Son of the Red Pirate" (U), 1.20, 5.5, 8.55; "Houdini" (U), L.P. 6.45. Thur.: "Prisoner of the Iron Mask" (U).

PICCADILLY, Sparkbrook * (ABC)—Judy Garland, Dirk Bogarde, "I Could Go On Singing" (U), 2.20, 5.30, 8.40; "Gang War" (A), 4.0, 7.15.

PICTURE House, Aston Cross (A.B.C.).—"Grip of Fear" (x), 4.30, 8.20; "Operation Mad Ball" (U) 6.35 (Mon. 2.50). Ads. Th.: "Manchurian Candidate" (A)

PLAZA, Stockland Green.— "Manchurian Candidate" (A), 2.30, 5.25, 8.25; "World of War" (U), 2.0, 5.0, 8.0. Th.: Elvis Presley. "Jailhouse Rock" (A)

PRINCES, SME. 0221.—Alan Ladd, "Shane" (U), 5.30, 8.40 (M. 2.15); "Young Captives" (A), 7.40 (M. 4.25). Thurs.: "Follow That Dream" (U)

ABC, Robin Hood, Hall Green. R. Hudson " Giant " (A) 12.45, 4.15, 7.40 Supp L.P. 7.10. Please note length. Thurs.: "Guns of the Black Witch" (A).

ROCK, Alum Rock. EAS. 0476. "Camp on Blood Island" (x), 2.20, 5.40, 8.55; "Gunman's Walk" (A). L.P. 7.10, adults. Th.: "Belles of St. Trinians" U.

ABC, Royalty, Harborne.— "Prisoner of the Iron Mask" (U), 3.10, 6.10, 9.10; "Journey to 7th Planet" U. L.P. 7.10 Th.: "Son of the Red Pirate" (U)

SHELDON *— Maurice Chevalier, Hayley Mills, "In Search of the Castaways" (U) (3.15 M. & W.), 5.55, 8.40. Supp. (2.20 M. & W.), 5.0, 7.35

SOLIHULL * SOL. 0398.—"Ben Hur" (A), One Perf. 6.55 (D.O. 6.25), Mat. Wed. 2.30, 5/-, 4/-, 3/-. Children Reduced Prices.

VICTORIA *, Victoria Road, Aston.— Charlton Heston, Jack Hawkins, "BEN HUR" (A). One performance Commencing 6.40.

VILLA CROSS * NOR. 0607.— Judy Garland, Dirk Bogarde, "I Could Go On Singing " (U). 2.10, 5.30, 8.45 (D.O. 1.50). "Gang War" (A). 4.0, 7.10.

WALDORF. Sparkbrook.— Patrick McGoohan, "The Quare Fellow" (x), Steve Cochran, "The Mobster" (x) Adults. Th.: "Lonely Are the Brave" (A).

ALDRIDGE CINEMA

AVION *—Stewart Granger, "SODOM AND GOMORRAH" (x) 4.30, 7.30 (Monday 1.40). Adults.

BLACKHEATH CINEMA

REX *— Elvis Presley, "KID GALAHAD" (U) 5.15, 8.49, (Monday 2.31). "FRONTIER UPRISING " (U) 7 16.

HALESOWEN CINEMA

LYTTLETON. HAL. 1448.— Cornel Wilde. "Constantine the Great" (A), 5.15, 8.36. "Mrs. Gibbons Boys" (A) 7.4. Th.: "Crooks Anonymous" U

LANGLEY CINEMA

REGENT. BRO. 1120.—"Mix Me a Person" (x) Adam Faith, 5.0, 8.36. "Don't Knock the Twist" (U), 7.0. Ad. Thurs.: "Belles of St. Trinians" (U).

WEST BROM. CINEMAS

QUEEN'S * WES. 0351.—" The White Slavers" (x) Etchika Choureau, 3.0, 5 40, 8.20. "The Wrestling Game" (A). 2.25, 5.10, 7.50. Adults.

ABC * WES. 1210. — Cliff Richard, Lauri Peters. "Summer Holiday" (U), 2.30, 5.30, 8.30. "Moment of Decision" (U) 1.30, 4.20, 7.20.

Hagley Road West/Harborne Road, Bearwood, 8th March 1963,

Grange Road/Avenue Road, Kings Heath, 1963.

Witton Lane/Park Road, Witton, 1963.

The City of Birmingham Symphony Orchestra depart for a tour of Germany and Switzerland, March 1963.

Oliver Street/Cromwell Street, Nechells, 1963.

The Queen arrives to see Bull Ring reconstruction work, 24th May 1963.

Some of the girls from Woolworths wait to catch a glimpse of Her Majesty.

The Dell, Kingshurst Hall Estate, Summer 1963.

Rear of Smith Street, Hockley, 5th June 1963.

Parade, 31st July 1963.

Published by REGIONAL PUBLICATIONS & DISPLAY LTD., 36, REGENT PLACE, BIRMINGHAM, 1.
Printed by THE BIRMINGHAM PRINTERS LTD., 42-44, HILL STREET, BIRMINGHAM, 5

The Congressmen, yet another of the City's busy beat groups.

All Saints Tavern, Lodge Road, Hockley, 1963.

The topping-out ceremony, performed by J.W. Barter, M.P., (left of centre) on the tenth floor of the North Birmingham Shopping Centre, Perry Barr, 24th September 1963. In August 1990 the One-Stop Shopping Centre opened on the same site.

Mr E.M. Clayson, Chairman of The Birmingham Post and Mail Ltd., with "Miss Kings Norton", Rita Bird, of Alvechurch Road, takes a spin in a dodgem car, Kings Norton Mop, The Green, 7th October 1963.

47

Fans waiting for the arrival of the Beatles, Hippodrome,
9th November 1963.

After the show the Beatles were smuggled out of the theatre,
disguised as policemen.

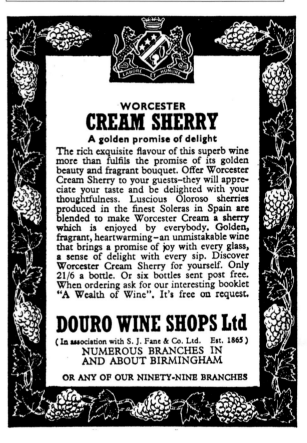

Kingstanding Road, Perry Barr, 19th December 1963.

Part of the interior of St Catherine of Siena Roman
Catholic Church, Bristol Street, January 1964.

Alcester Road South, Maypole, 30th January 1964.

Edgewood Road, Rednal, 1964.

The Dutch Swing College Orchestra appears at the
Town Hall, 11th February 1964.

High Street, from the Rotunda, 1964.

Wheelwright Road, Erdington, 2nd April 1964.

Suggestion scheme prizewinners, Joseph Lucas Ltd., Sparkhill, c 1964.

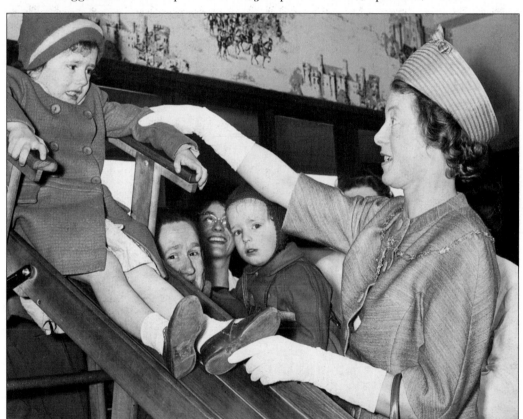

Bernadette Holmes receives a helping hand from the Lady Mayoress, Mrs L. Glass, Nechells Green Health Welfare Centre, 13th April 1964.

51

The Lord Mayor, Ald. Louis Glass, speaks, through a specially-adapted system, to children at the Longwill School for the Deaf, Bell Hill, Northfield, 5th May 1964.

Gill Merrick, Birmingham City F.C. and England goalkeeper, seen here in the fifties, went on to become the Blues manager from 1960 to 1964.

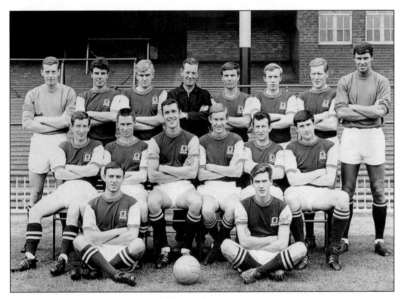

Aston Villa F.C., 1963/4.

After the official opening of the Bull Ring Centre, the Duke of Edinburgh meets some of the spectators, 29th May 1964.

Golden Hillock Road/Sydenham Road, Sparkhill, 16th June 1964.

Electrical shop, Midland Red, Carlyle Works, Edgbaston, 1964.

Old Oscott Lane/Dyas Road, Kingstanding, 22nd July 1964.

Church Road, Yardley, 22nd July 1964.

Turfpits Lane, with Short Heath Road on the left, Erdington, 23rd July 1964.

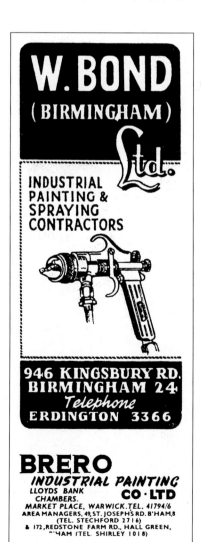

New Street/Corporation Street, 30th July 1964.

An RAF trainer on display in the Bull Ring Centre, c 1964.

Aston Street/Sheep Street, Aston, 9th September 1964.

Actor, Tony Britton, goes for a double top, in the pub where his father was landlord during the depression years, The Royal Mint, Icknield Street, Hockley, 20th September 1964.

Gracie Fields struts her stuff, Town Hall, 24th September 1964.

Roger Tonge, Jill Rossington and Noele Gordon, in the first episode of "Crossroads", 2nd November 1964.

Taylor Street/Bloomsbury Street, Nechells Green, 10th November 1964.

Bristol Road South, Northfield, 6th November 1964.

The Lord Mayor, Ald. Frank Price, plants the first poppy in the Remembrance Sunday ceremony, Bull Ring, November 1964.

Leopold Street, Highgate, 14th December 1964.

Corporation Street, 21st December 1964.

Denise Carpenter, from Nechells, meets Father Christmas, Co-op, High Street, 1964.

Farren Road/Tessall Lane, Northfield, 1964.

The first major winter sale starts, Lewis's, 30th December 1964.

1965

Oxhill Road, Handsworth, 18th February 1965.

Highgate Road, Sparkbrook, 9th March 1965.

Booths Farm Road/Perry Wood Road, Perry Barr, 2nd April 1965.

Heathfield Road, Handsworth, 29th April 1965.

Cromwell Hall F.C., Winson Green, c 1965.

Lindsworth Approach/Monyhull Hall Road,
Kings Norton, 4th May 1965.

Kings Road, Kingstanding, 15th May 1965.

Brook Lane, Kings Heath, 31st May 1965.

Soho Road/Murdoch Road, Handsworth, 2nd June 1965.

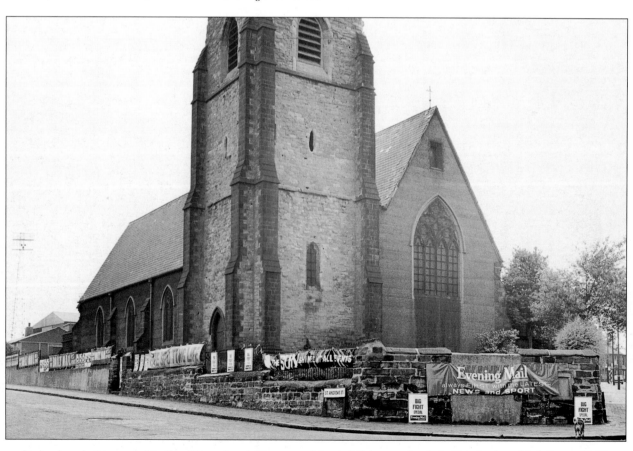

St Andrew's Street, with the Blues football ground just visible on the left, Bordesley, 18th June 1965.

William Cook Road/Washwood Heath Road, Ward End, 13th July 1965.

Lench Street/Loveday Street, 15th July 1965.

Manzoni Gardens, St Martin's Circus, with the Rotunda on the right, July 1965.

Some of the stars featured in the 200th anniversary programme of ABC's "Thank Your Lucky Stars". The group includes Helen Shapiro, The Seekers, Mark Wynter, Mike Sarne, Jim Dale, Brian Matthews, Pete Murray, Janice Nicholls, Jackie Crier and the Lucky Stars Dancers, 17th July 1965.

Perrott's Folly, Edgbaston, c 1965.

Highfield Road, Hall Green, 1965.

Cheatham Street/Nechells Park Road, 23rd July 1965.

Macdonald Street Service Station, Highgate, August 1965.

Washington Street/Gough Street, off Holloway Head, 3rd August 1965.

Walsall Road, Perry Barr, 3rd August 1965.

Queueing to see the exhibition of "Dr Who and the Daleks" ephemera, Lewis's, 1965.

Granville Street/Ridley Street, Lee Bank, 1965.

Demolition work taking place from the top of the Norwich Union building in Congreve Street, looking across towards Baskerville House, 31st August 1965.

A NEW landmark rose on the
Birmingham skyline — one
which, by general agreement
gave a building truly worthy of
the Second City.

It was the £7,500,000 home of the
Birmingham Post & Mail Ltd. — moved
from the historic New Street - Cannon
Street site.

So impressed was Lord Snowdon, when
he came with Princes Margaret for the
Royal opening in October that he asked
for detailed plans and photographs of this
super · modern newspaper centre — having a special interest as honorary adviser
to the Council of Industrial Design — to
be sent to him.

Reservoir Road/Osler Street, Ladywood, 25th October 1965.

Warwick Road, Sparkhill, 1965.

Winson Green Road, with Heath Street at the traffic lights, July 1965.

Great Russell Street, Newtown, 8th November 1965.

Coventry Road, Sheldon, 17th December 1965.

1966

INFORMATION FOR MOTORISTS

Motor Taxation Office: Oozells Street. CENtral 9944.
  Driving Licences: Oozells Street. CENtral 9944.
*Royal Automobile Club, 93/95 Hagley Road, Edgbaston, 16.
  EDGbaston 5401.
*Automobile Association, 111 Hagley Road, 16. EDGbaston 6121.
  Blue Star Garages Ltd., 2 Pershore Street, 5. MIDland 2397.
†Pearce Service Garage, Gt. Charles Street, 3. CENtral 8035.
  Rootes Ltd., 90 Charlotte Street, 3. CENtral 8411.
†Smithfield Garage, Digbeth, 5. MIDland 4577.
  Somerset House Garage, Temple Street, 2. MIDland 2615.
*Twenty-four hour Service
⁺ Twenty-four hour Service except Saturday and Sunday.

Municipal Car Parks
  Bartholomew Row (Cars and Coaches)
  Civic Centre
  St. Chad's Circus   7.30 a.m.   Unmanned
  Lancaster Place; Corporation Street;   to   Sundays
  Snow Hill; Summer Row   7.30 p.m.
  Dudley Street Ringway Underground   7. a.m.—2.30 a.m.   Closed
  Holliday Street, West End   7.30 a.m.—12.45 a.m.   Sundays

Private Car Parks
  Bull Ring Centre Autopark (Ring Road, south carriageway) MIDland 1186
  Bull Ring Multi-Storey Car Park (Park Street) MIDland 0243
  Pearce Autopark, Cornwall Street, 3. CENtral 8035

24-hour service Central Garages
  Blue Star Garages Ltd., 2 Pershore Street, 5   MIDland 2397
  Rootes Ltd., 90 Charlotte Street, 3   CENtral 8411

The Post Office Tower (now known as the
BT Tower) Newhall Street, 1966. It was
officially opened on the 5th October 1967.

Bath Street, 1966.

Tyburn Road, Erdington, 4th February 1966.

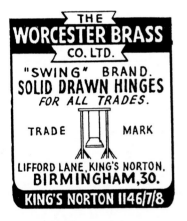

The Ritz Bingo Hall, Bordesley Green East/Little Bromwich Road, 17th March 1966.

Nechells Place/Nechells Park Road, 25th April 1966.

Warren Farm Road, Kingstanding, 14th April 1966.

Maryland Avenue, Ward End, 1966.

Pitney Street, Vauxhall, 26th April 1966.

A courtyard off High Park Street, Nechells, 25th April 1966.

Soho Hill, with Hamstead Road first on the right, 1966.

Aston Street, with the quaintly-shaped Warwick Castle Public House on the right, 7th June 1966.

Bristol Road South, Northfield, 23rd June 1966.

College Road, Handsworth, 8th August 1966.

Furnace Lane, Lozells, 1966.

Rear of the Saracen's Head, Kings Norton Green, 1966.

Danny King and the Mayfair Set, c 1966.

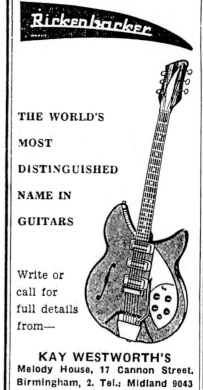

Aston Junction, Mill Street, 3rd August 1966.

Mike Smith holds the Gillette Cup won by Warwickshire C.C.C. at Lords, 3rd September 1966.
They beat Worcestershire by five wickets.

Kingsbury Road, Erdington, 23rd September 1966.

Wheeler Street, Newtown, October 1966.

A view from Bath Row, along the Birmingham and Worcester Canal, 1966.

Farm Street/Gee Street, Hockley, 5th December 1966.

Hobmoor Road, with Rostrevor Road on the right, Small Heath, 1966.

Botanical Gardens, Edgbaston, December 1966.

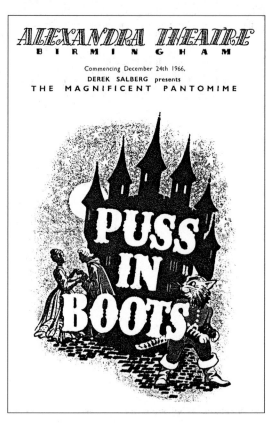

Des O'Connor

Rikki Fulton

Jean Barrington

Stars of the Alexandra's pantomime.

1967

Weldall & Co. (Small Heath) Ltd., Somerville Road, between St Benedict's Road and Heather Road, February 1967.

Albert Road/Park Road, Aston, 1967.

Hope Street, Highgate, 13th February 1967.

Rear of St Martin's Street, Edgbaston, 1967.

Rear of Key Hill, Hockley, 1967.

The Polish Catholic Association, Bordesley Street, 1967.

Clearing the wreckage of the train crash at
Stechford Station, 28th February 1967.

Rear of Gee Street, Newtown, 8th March 1967.

Corporation Baths and Dr Gattas's surgery, Monument Road,
Ladywood, c 1967.

Jane Fyffe.

The Overhead Department (opposite Miller Street tram depot),
Aston –

– and as demolition takes place, 1967.

St Martin's Street/William Street, Edgbaston, April 1967.

Shooting continues on the film, "Privilege", with a blow-up picture of Paul Jones dominating the brass band scene, filmed at St Andrew's football ground, 18th April 1967.

Rea Street/Cheapside, 10th July 1967.

King Edward's Road, with Alexandra Street in the centre, Ladywood, 1967.

The Rover Co. Ltd., Lee Crescent/Ryland Road, Lee Bank, 1967.

Chandos Junior and Infant School, Moseley Road, Highgate, July 1967.

Clifton Road, Sparkbrook, 14th July 1967.

Bull Ring, 1st August 1967.

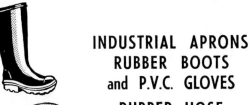

Swinford Road, Selly Oak, 1967.

Members of Moseley CC who played in all five Championship years from 1956 – 1967, R.B. Abbell, J.W. Thompson, D.M.W. Heath, H.J. Latham and G. Jakeman.

Martin Hone, owner of the Opposite Lock, in Gas Street, takes part in ABC TV's "Strictly for Laughs", 22nd August 1967. The programme was chaired by Kenneth Horne and involved members of the public competing with professional comics.

Holliday Street/Granville Street, August 1967.

Lawrence Street, Gosta Green, 8th September 1967.

Englehard Industries Ltd., Vyse Street, Jewellery Quarter, 1967.

Weoley Castle Road, October 1967.

The Green, Kings Norton, 11th October 1967.

Hawthorn Road, Kingstanding, 1967.

Firemen attend a fire at Hanger's car showrooms, Broad Street, 7th November 1967.

North Birmingham Shopping Centre, Perry Barr, 15th November 1967.

Gerrard Street/Wheeler Street, Newtown, 11th December 1967.

Summer Road/Fox Hollies Road, Acocks Green, January 1968.

The first customers arrive for the January sale, C. & A. Modes, Corporation Street, 2nd January 1968.

Coventry Road, between Golden Hillock Road and Wordsworth Road, Small Heath, January 1968.

Lancaster Circus, 9th January 1968.

Auchinleck Square, Broad Street, Five Ways, 19th January 1968.

The Lord Mayor, Ald. James Meadows, makes a
spectacular entrance into the Bull Ring Centre,
25th January 1968.

Craelius Co. Ltd., (diamond core and concrete drilling manufacturers) Cheston Road, Aston, 4th February 1968.

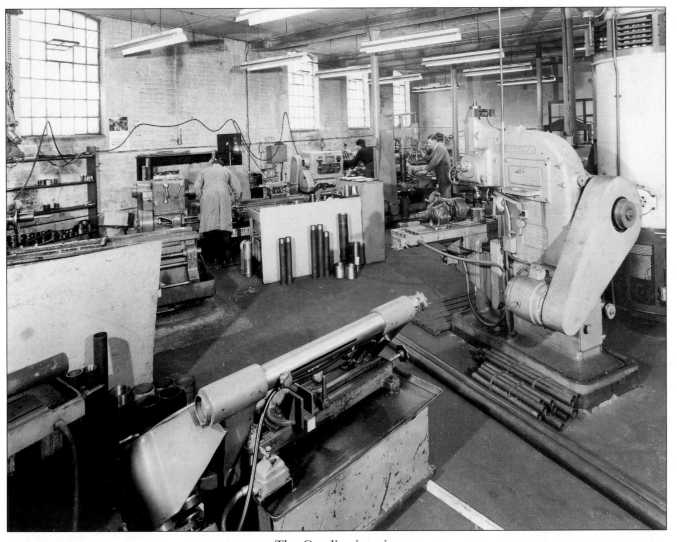

The Craelius interior.

Summer Row, 1968.

Morchard Place, off Ryland Road, Lee Bank, 6th March 1968.

Clark Street/Reservoir Road, Ladywood, 21st March 1968.

Evergreen Walk, rear of 5 Devon Street, Nechells, 1968.

Balsall Heath Road/Longbridge Road, 1968.

A fine view of the old and the new, showing Big Brum, Galloways Corner still intact, and the Rotunda completed, 29th April 1968.

Stockfield Road, Acocks Green, 25th June 1968.

Turner Street, Sparkbrook, 1968.

P.L. Trickett (motor engineers and garage) Beeches Road/Trehurst Avenue, Great Barr, 11th June 1968.

Steelhouse Lane, with the General Hospital on the right, 20th August 1968.

Tyseley Railway Museum, Summer 1968.

BIRMINGHAM THEATRE

Proprietors	MOSS EMPIRES LTD.
Chairman	PRINCE LITTLER, C.B.E.
Managing Director	LESLIE A. MACDONNELL, O.B.E.
Resident Musical Director	GWYN DAVIES

| Manager & Licensee | .. .. | WILFRED MAY |
| House Manager | .. .. | BARRY HOPSON |

Phone : 021-622 2576

TUESDAY, SEPTEMBER 26th
for 7 weeks
6.15   TWICE NIGHTLY   8.30

PRICES OF ADMISSION

	Mon. to Fri.	Saturday
Boxes	35/- 45/-	40/- 50/-
Orchestra Stalls	10/6	12/6
Stalls	6/6 9/-	8/- 11/-
Dress Circle	10/6	12/6
Circle	4/6 6/- 9/-	5/6 7/6 11/-

Box Office open 10 a.m. to 9 p.m.

LESLIE A. MACDONNELL
announces that

ROBERT LUFF Holdings Ltd.
(in assoc. with GEORGE MITCHELL)
present

THE
BLACK
& WHITE
MINSTREL
SHOW

BASED ON THE POPULAR B.B.C.-T.V. SERIES

Vocal arrangements and routines by
GEORGE MITCHELL

Choreography by	Lighting by
LARRY GORDON and	LAURIE BLOOM
ROY GUNSON	

| Costumes designed by | Decor by |
| R. ST. JOHN ROPER | BRUCE PALMER |

Devised and produced by GEORGE INNS

PHOTOGRAPHING IN THE THEATRE IS FORBIDDEN
The Management reserve the right to refuse admission to this
theatre, and to change, vary or omit, without previous notice,
any item of the programme.

GLYN DAWSON

FREDDY WILLIAMS

PETER DARREN

THE MITCHELL MINSTRELS

The last building in the street to be demolished,
Carrs Lane/Moor Street, 1968.

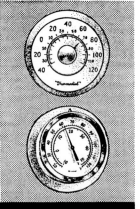

Ladywood M.P., Victor Yates, talks to Mrs Doreen Brenner about the terrible housing conditions suffered by her and many of his constituents, Spring Hill, 28th September 1968.

107

Rear of Potter's Hill, Aston, 1968.

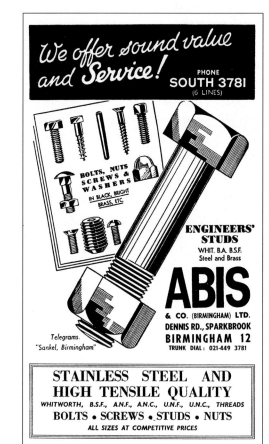

T H I R D

MOSELEY & KINGS HEATH
HORTICULTURAL SOCIETY

LATE CHRYSANTHEMUM **SHOW**
Nov. 1968

HANDICRAFT SECTION

Class No. 43. Metalwork, Small Pewter or Copper Article

Name Mrs A. Jennings,

Address 309, Greathorpe Rd, Birmingham, 29.

Entry No. 52

Soho Road, with Rookery Road coming up on the right, Handsworth, 1968.

The Queen Mother signs the visitor's book, after attending the consecration service at the Parish Church of St Peter, Tile Cross, 13th November 1968. The vicar of St Peter's, The Rev. A.J. Draper (left) and the Bishop of Birmingham, the Rt. Rev. Dr. J.L. Wilson, look on.

The Lord Mayor and Lady Mayoress, Ald. and Mrs Charles Simpson, throw an eighth birthday party for their son, Alexander, Council House, 12th January 1969.

CRIME COUNT

Offences reported in Birmingham in the past week.

POLICE DIVISION	BURGLARIES	CAR THEFTS	THEFTS FROM CARS	VIOLENCE
A City Centre.	8	13	7	4
B Cotteridge, Harborne, Kings Norton, Longbridge, Northfield, Selly Oak, Selly Park, West Heath.	13	17	13	4
C Bearwood, Edgbaston, Handsworth, Ladywood, Lozells, Winson Green.	49	17	6	5
D Aston, Birchfields, Castle Vale, Erdington, Great Barr, Kingstanding, Newtown, Perry Barr, Witton.	42	20	12	7
E Acocks Green, Bordesley Green, Hay Mills, Sheldon, Small Heath, Stechford, Ward End, Washwood Heath, Yardley.	30	27	12	9
F Balsall Heath, Hall Green, Highters Heath, King's Heath, Moseley, Sparkbrook, Sparkhill, Tyseley, Warstock, Yardley Wood.	19	18	11	4
WEEK'S TOTAL	161	112	61	33

Administration Section, Wesleyan and General Assurance Society, Colmore Circus, 1969.

The Ladywood Middleway is under construction, with Spring Hill Library on the right of the picture, c 1969.

The Lord Mayor, Ald. Charles Simpson, toasts the health of the members at the opening of the city's Nautical Club, Dean Street, 15th March 1969.

Staff at St Vincent's R.C. Primary School, Nechells, 1969.

Athletic teams, St Vincent's R.C. Primary School,
Vauxhall Grove, Nechells, July 1969 –

– and swimming teams.

Ann Jones, another proud daughter of the city,
wins Wimbledon, July 1969.

AND so the thing has been done at last. We have walked the moon.

It is so great a step that words falter. For the first time, man has trodden an alien world.

We have broken down the barriers which for more than 1,000,000 years have confined us to this earth.

For this we owe a great debt to the United States. Nothing could have been more perfect than the technical progress of the moon landing.

A newly-established patrol force using transport similar to the police panda car, maintaining contact with headquarters by radio and, where necessary, accompanied by a trained Alsatian guard dog is now operating in the City Parks and Recreation Grounds.

Recruits to the new force are given intensive training in the law relating to parks, and a number of instructional sessions at the Police Training School.

The patrols' main duty is to ensure that bye-laws are observed so that the parks may be enjoyed by all, to check vandalism and hooliganism and now, having made a declaration before a Justice of the Peace with powers of arrest in the parks, members of the force should be able to deal with most cases of bad behaviour in the parks.

So far, the number of sales of Corporation houses completed or in progress numbers 4,362.

By Government Order, Birmingham has to restrict the sale of Corporation houses to about 350 a year, and it seems likely that the 1969/70 quota of sales will have been used up by the end of the year. This being so, no further sales will be possible until the 1st August 1970, when the next quota becomes available.

Birmingham's seventh Municipal Golf Course has been opened at Hatchford Brook on the Coventry Road near Birmingham Airport.

This 18-hole course has been laid out on some 150 acres of land and for the initiated has a par of 69 for its 6,226 yards length.

A large number of hedgerow trees have been retained and incorporated in the course layout, and extensive planting of semi-mature trees has also taken place.

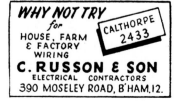

Gerrard Street, Lozells, c 1969.

Hingeston Street, Hockley, c 1969.

Church Lane, Aston, 9th September 1969.

Church Lane, Aston, 10th September 1969.

Mark and Steven Davies enjoy the Kings Norton
Mop, October 1969.

All Saints Street/All Saints Road, Hockley, 1969.

R.M. Douglas Asphalt and Paving Ltd., George Road, Erdington, 27th October 1969.

Gravelly Hill interchange, from Copeley Hill, Erdington, October 1969.

Newport Road, Sparkbrook, 1969.

Part of the Inner Ring Road, running up to Great Charles Street, 15th November 1969.

Bristol Road South, Northfield, 3rd December 1969.

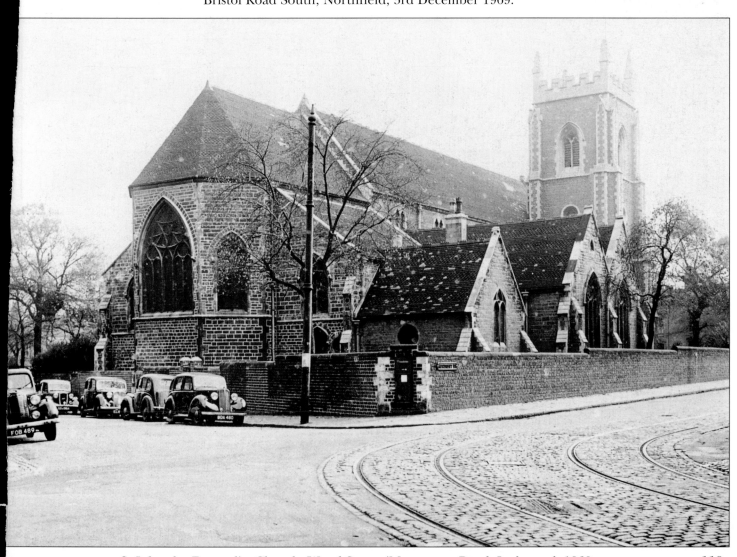

St John the Evangelist Church, Wood Street/Monument Road, Ladywood, 1969.

Back Cover: Jamaica Row, 21st December 1964.

ACKNOWLEDGEMENTS
(for providing photographs, for encouragement and numerous other favours)

Jim & Pete Addison; Ambleside Garden Centre, Earlswood; The Birmingham City Council Dept. of Planning and Architecture; The Birmingham Post and Mail Ltd.; Nell Blackburn; Charlie and Nora Bottrill; Marjorie Braines; David Broadbent; Hilda Broadbent; Anne Cannell; Dave and Kath Carpenter; Dave Coles; Mark Davies; John Enticknap; David Fleming; Joyce Gill; David Goodyear; The Hay Loft, Boxtrees Farm, Hockley Heath; International Print Shop; Anne Jennings; Dave, Thelma and Tom Jones; Joyce Lockwood; Betty Milne; Dennis Moore; Maude Nicklin; Northfield Books & Models; Janet Owen; George Peace; Douglas Price; Anne Randle; Keith Shakespeare; Keith Smart; Travel West Midlands; Joan Wanty; Joan Ward; Ron Ward; Warwickshire C.C.C.; Joan Wilkes; Rosemary Wilkes; Keith and Mo Williams.

Please forgive any possible omissions. Every effort has been made to include all organisations and individuals in the book.

The Lord Mayor and Lady Mayoress, Ald. and Mrs E.W. Horton, with the children of employees of Birmingham City Transport, at a party and circus at Wheelers Lane Sports Ground, Kings Heath, 15th August 1962.